The CIA

The CIA

Brendan January

Franklin Watts
A Division of Scholastic Inc.
New York • Toronto • London • Auckland • Sydney
Mexico City • New Delhi • Hong Kong
Danbury, Connecticut

Note to readers: Definitions for words in **bold** can be found in the Glossary at the back of this book.

The photograph on the cover shows a computer operator working at the CIA headquarters in Langley, Virginia. The photograph opposite the title page shows a CIA staff member examining the robotic arm of a computer storage device.

Photographs © 2002: AP/Wide World Photos: 22 (Allied Museum), 52, 53 (J. Scott Applewhite), 41 (Raul Corrales/Granma/Canadian Press Photo), 24 (Federation of American Scientists), 32, 33 (Pablo Martinez Monsivais), 26, 48, 49; Archive Photos/Getty Images: 51 (Win McNamee/Reuters), 6 (Scott Swanson); Brown Brothers: 9; Corbis Images: 40, 50 (AFP), 25, 31, 37, 42, 43, 44, 46 (Bettman), 36 (Hulton-Deutsch Collection), cover, 2, 5 right, 13, 14 (Roger Ressmeyer), 10, 34; Folio, Inc./Michael Patrick: 15; Hulton|Archive/Getty Images: 11; NASA: 5 left, 23; PictureQuest/N. Malyshev/Sovfoto/Eastfoto: 19; Superstock, Inc.: 16.

Library of Congress Cataloging-in-Publication Data

January, Brendan, 1972-
    The CIA / Brendan January.
        p. cm.
    Includes bibliographical references and index.
    Summary: Introduces the history, organization, and mission of the Central Intelligence Agency.
    ISBN 0-531-12034-1 (lib. bdg.) 0-531-16600-7 (pbk.)
    1. United States. Central Intelligence Agency—Juvenile literature. [1. United States. Central Intelligence Agency. 2. Intelligence service. 3. Spies.] 1. Title: Central Intelligence Agency. II. Title.

JK468.I6 J36 2002
327.1273—dc21   2001004964

Contents

The CIA was born after the disastrous surprise attack on Pearl Harbor on December 7, 1941. Here, the Shaw burns as fire crews spray the decks of the battleship Nevada *(at right).*

Chapter One

Born in Fire

In the early light of December 7, 1941, six Japanese aircraft carriers launched more than 350 warplanes. They formed into groups and flew south toward Pearl Harbor, Hawaii, home to the main American naval base in the Pacific Ocean. Six battleships, the pride of the American fleet, were docked in two rows. Around 8:00 A.M., the first Japanese planes swooped over the harbor, dropping torpedoes and bombs. At first, many Americans thought it was a practice drill. Then explosions began to tear through the battleships. The American sailors and soldiers were completely surprised.

The attack lasted less than two hours. When the Japanese planes finally disappeared, Pearl Harbor lay shattered. One battleship had blown up and was covered in flames. Another had rolled over, its dripping propellers pointed to the sky. Several other ships had sunk to the bottom of the harbor. Twisted metal, charred debris, and bodies were scattered in the water and on nearby airfields. The air above Pearl Harbor was choked with billowing smoke. With one blow, more than two thousand Americans had been killed and the U.S. Pacific fleet had been crippled. The next day, the United States declared war on Japan and entered World War II.

After the shock of the attack faded, Americans began angrily asking questions: Had there been any signs that the Japanese were about to attack? Why had we been so unprepared? How did we get taken by surprise?

The disaster at Pearl Harbor showed a serious weakness in the nation's defenses. The United States did not have a strong, well-organized group to gather information, to detect danger, and to warn the nation's leaders of threats to national security. The country needed a central **intelligence** service.

The Office of Strategic Services

Why was intelligence so important? In the jungles and islands of the Pacific, in northern Europe and Africa, and on the plains of Russia, millions of men were locked in battle during World War II. It would take more than soldiers, guns, and bullets to win the war. It would take information.

During World War II, intelligence came from many sources. Photographs taken from aircraft showed the locations of enemy factories, tanks, and forts. Codebreakers intercepted and read enemy messages, and spies revealed secret plans. Good intelligence saved lives, equipment, and supplies—and it was often the difference between victory and defeat.

To create an American intelligence service, President Franklin Delano Roosevelt turned to a decorated war veteran and lawyer, General William "Wild Bill" Donovan. In 1942,

U.S. Marines get ready for battle on the southwestern Pacific island of Saipan during World War II. In the background, a landing craft burns after being hit by Japanese artillery.

9

In 1942, General William "Wild Bill" Donovan became head of the Office of Strategic Services, the intelligence organization that grew into the CIA.

President Roosevelt named Donovan director of a new intelligence organization, the Office of Strategic Services (OSS). Under the executive branch of government, the OSS worked with the U.S. Army and Navy to gather information on the war. The OSS also mounted secret operations to spread confusion and disrupt the enemy. These operations were called **covert action**.

The OSS dropped teams behind enemy lines, smuggled arms to resistance groups, and recruited Nazi spies. Donovan took a look at any plan that might weaken the enemy, no matter how strange or incredible. He even considered using bats to drop bombs on Tokyo, the Japanese capital city.

Time for the CIA

After the war ended in 1945, President Harry Truman disbanded the OSS. During times of peace, he reasoned, the country did not need to gather intelligence or to spy on other countries. Soon, however, a new threat loomed—this one from the Soviet Union. At the end of World War II, the Soviet armies had driven through the countries of Eastern Europe—Poland, Romania, Hungary, Yugoslavia, Czechoslovakia, and East Germany—and had installed or supported a **communist** government in each.

After World War II ended, President Harry Truman turned the eyes of U.S. intelligence toward a new threat: communism. Here, Soviet troops sweep into Prague, Czechoslovakia, on May 9, 1945.

The Americans and the British angrily protested the Soviets' action. When Truman tried to respond to the Soviets, however, he found it difficult to get accurate information. No one could tell him what they were really doing or predict what they would do in the future. No one knew the strength of the Soviet armies and their weapons. Some Americans feared another devastating surprise attack like the one at Pearl Harbor.

Truman now realized that disbanding the OSS had been a mistake. Even during peacetime, he needed information to make decisions. U.S. lawmakers also saw the Soviets as a new threat. In 1947, Congress passed the National Security Act, which created an organization to gather and sort through information: the Central Intelligence Agency (CIA).

Today's Intelligence

Today, more than fifty years after it was founded, the CIA is the largest intelligence agency in the world. About 22,000 people work for the CIA, most of them at its headquarters in Langley, Virginia. The agency is divided into four groups called directorates: Operations, Science and Technology, Intelligence, and Administration.

The Directorate of Operations gathers information through secret operations, including the use of spies. CIA operations officers are Americans who recruit **agents** from other countries. Agents give the officers **classified** information such as statistics, plans, documents, and letters.

12

The Directorate of Science and Technology uses technology to gather information. Its staff watch other countries through powerful cameras mounted in satellites and aircraft. They listen to radio messages and translate foreign broadcasts and newspapers. Finally, they develop new technology, such as recording devices that are smaller than a penny.

The Directorate of Intelligence sorts through the information gathered by the first two directorates by translating it into easily understood reports and passing it on to the right people. Its staff are experts on other countries, including their culture,

CIA staff get tae kwon do instruction during their lunch hour at the CIA headquarters.

A staff member at the CIA Office of Imagery Analysis studies images of SAM-2 missiles. The information he gathers will eventually reach the Directorate of Intelligence.

language, and government. Drawing on this knowledge, they make predictions about how a leader or a country will act.

Because it is so powerful, the CIA is often the target of rival spy operations. The Directorate of Administration provides security for the agency. It scans CIA buildings for spy equipment such as **bugs** and wiretaps. It also looks out for CIA officers who might sell agency secrets.

A Secret Organization

While recruiting and managing spies and agents, CIA officers sometimes break the laws of other countries. If discovered, agents can lose their lives. The CIA performs most of its work in secrecy. When its leaders report to Congress, they speak in a closed, soundproof chamber. The organization's budget is not reported to the public. Even the CIA's headquarters, a 258-acre (104-hectare) compound outside Washington, D.C., was not marked on nearby road signs until recent years.

The CIA's tendency toward secrecy has given the agency an image problem. CIA officers sometimes make serious mistakes and break the law, but the agency rarely comments to the press or explains its actions. Faced with silence, people have blamed the CIA for many things, from UFOs to assassinations to the AIDS virus. As CIA officers frequently point out, the agency's successes are never known, but its failures are published everywhere.

CIA headquarters in Langley, Virginia

Winston Churchill, Harry S. Truman, and Joseph Stalin—known as the Big Three—meet in Potsdam, Germany, in 1945. With the end of a world war, a new conflict began: the Cold War.

Chapter Two

Looking Over the Iron Curtain

The CIA was established at the beginning of the **Cold War**. This was the period from 1945 to about 1990, when the United States and the Soviet Union struggled to dominate the world. The war was described as "cold" because the gigantic American and Soviet armies never battled each other. Instead, the two countries fought through covert action and **espionage**, or spying. In the Cold War, wrote U.S. Lieutenant James Doolittle, "There are no rules. . . . Fair play has no place in this deadly game."

To many CIA officers, the Cold War was about good against evil. The Soviet Union was characterized as evil because it did not grant the freedoms that Americans enjoyed, such as freedoms of speech, press, and religion. During the 1930s, Soviet citizens had lived in terror of their own police and government leaders, who arrested, imprisoned, and killed millions of Soviet people.

The Iron Curtain

The CIA's first mission in the Cold War was to learn about the Soviet Union, a giant, secretive nation that covered one-sixth of the world's land surface. Like the United States, the Soviet Union had entered World War II after a devastating surprise attack, this one by German armies that had smashed into Soviet territory. After the war, Soviet leader Joseph Stalin vowed that his nation would never again be taken by surprise. As a result, the Soviet secret police were asked to keep tight control over the people. Soon even the Moscow phone book became classified information.

In a speech delivered in 1946, British prime minister Winston Churchill warned that the Soviet Union had drawn an "iron curtain" across Europe, and nothing could be seen over or through it. Because of this "iron curtain," the CIA had no knowledge of the size of the Soviet armies, the number of

Soviet factories, the amount of grain its farmers grew, or the layout of its railroads. In the United States, people could drive almost anywhere they wanted and freely take photographs. In the Soviet Union, such action was immediately suspicious and could lead to imprisonment.

Hoping to see the Soviet landscape, the CIA launched thousands of what it called "weather balloons," which were spy devices equipped with cameras. The balloons drifted at an altitude of 50,000 feet (15,250 meters) across the Soviet Union, took pictures, and then ejected their film by parachute. Following a radio signal, American aircraft retrieved the film. This program was unsuccessful, however. Of the 516 balloons used, only 41 returned safely. Many landed or were shot down in Poland and the Soviet Union, where outraged Soviet officials placed them on display.

The CIA did learn something from an unlikely source—a coat hanger. In Austria, an agent found a Soviet coat hanger buried in trash. The hanger was

Russian Rival

The CIA faced a formidable enemy in the Soviet intelligence and secret police, called the Komitet Gosundarstuennoy Bezopasnosti (KGB). Like the CIA, the KGB collected vast amounts of information, but unlike its American counterpart, the KGB itself did not analyze intelligence. Instead, it sent the information on to government leaders, who personally examined it.

made from metal pieces left over from the construction of a new Soviet bomber. In Washington, D.C., experts closely examined the metal. Through a series of tests, they were able to calculate how many bombs the airplane could carry and how far it could fly.

U-2

In the late 1950s, the CIA was finally able to peek over the iron curtain. In 1954, CIA officer Richard Bissell began developing a new aircraft. He sought to build a plane that flew so high and so fast that it could soar over the Soviet Union, higher than Soviet fighters and missiles could reach.

After just eighteen months, the new airplane, called the U-2, took its first test flight. With a 79-foot (24-m) wingspan, the U-2 could cruise at almost 70,000 feet (21,350 m). The plane's cameras could record images of objects measuring only inches across. On one test flight over the United States, the U-2 took photographs of President Dwight D. Eisenhower playing golf. When Eisenhower saw the pictures, he was delighted. He authorized the first flight.

On July 4, 1956, the U-2 took off from an airbase in England. It crossed into Soviet airspace and took a bold route directly over Moscow, the Soviet capital. Soviet fighter planes and antiaircraft weapons could not reach the U-2. Embarrassed, the Soviets quietly protested to the United States. After all, the U-2 flight had blatantly broken international law. Eisenhower ordered more flights, however, and the CIA continued to break the law under the direction of the president.

With the U-2, the CIA was at last able to gather much of the information it had been seeking. After examining millions of photographs, CIA analysts realized that the Soviet Union did not have as many missiles as the Americans had feared. Top American officials were relieved.

The U-2 missions ultimately led to disaster, however. In 1960, President Eisenhower was scheduled to meet with the Soviet leader, Nikita Khrushchev, in a summit designed to smooth relations between the two countries. The CIA requested one last U-2 scouting flight. Officials assured the president that the Soviets still could not shoot down the plane—and even if they did, the pilot would either die or commit suicide. Eisenhower gave the order.

On May 1, 1960, the U-2, piloted by Gary Powers, streaked into Soviet airspace. The Soviets spotted the U-2 and launched a new, powerful missile at the high-flying craft. The

missile missed the plane but flew close enough to cause the U-2's delicate wing to buckle. The aircraft crashed to the earth while Powers parachuted to safety. The Soviets found the smoldering wreckage and captured Powers.

At first, Eisenhower denied that the U-2 even existed. Then the Soviets revealed Powers to the world, and the president was caught in an embarrassing lie. Khrushchev canceled the meeting with Eisenhower, and the opportunity to discuss peace was gone.

Eyes in the Sky

The CIA followed up the U-2's success with another aircraft, the SR-71 Blackbird. Flying at a speed of more than 2,000 miles (3,200 kilometers) per hour, the SR-71 could reach an altitude of 85,000 feet (25,900 km). Within 1 hour, it could photograph 100,000 square miles (259,000 square km) of land.

Soon the agency was reaching even higher. In 1959, the CIA launched the first of the Corona Satellites, which were fired into the atmosphere on a rocket. They orbited Earth once every 95 minutes and took pictures of the terrain. The

The SR-71 Blackbird was a new, improved spy plane developed by the CIA during the Cold War. Today, SR-71s are used for aeronautical research.

This photograph, taken by a U.S. spy satellite during the Cold War, shows a weapons facility in Sverdlovsk, Russia.

satellites then ejected the film by parachute, and airplanes caught the film in midflight.

Today, spy satellites are always orbiting the Earth. The latest versions, the KH-11 and KH-12 satellites, cost more than $1 billion each. Orbiting at more than 200 miles (320 km) above Earth's surface, these satellites use cameras powerful enough to read a license-plate number.

It's Cold in Asia, Too

In the mid-twentieth century, the CIA extended its Cold War effort to a new frontier—Asia. In 1949, communist leader Mao Zedong seized power in China. The United States decided to resist any further expansion of communism into countries along the Pacific Ocean. That decision was tested on June 24, 1950, when North Korean tanks and soldiers poured into South Korea in a surprise attack.

American leaders criticized the CIA for not warning them of North Korea's plans, even though the agency had in fact noted a troop buildup in North Korea. One person called the

24

CIA's effort a "well-intentioned flop." General Walter Bedell Smith, who had become CIA director, complained that leaders' expectations of the agency were too high. "They expect you to able to say that a war will start next Tuesday at 5:32 P.M.," he said. It was clear, however, that the agency had failed to provide a strong enough warning.

United Nations officials inspect North Korean troops during the Korean War in the 1950s.

CIA director Allen Dulles was the mastermind behind the agency's intelligence structure. Today that structure includes stations in 130 countries.

Chapter Three

Officers, Agents, and Spies

The CIA's intelligence structure was put in place by Allen Dulles, who took over as director in 1952. Today, the CIA maintains stations in 130 countries. The size of the stations varies from one person to more than fifty. The officers at the stations watch the nation's economy, the society at large, and the people who hold power. In simple terms, their job is to know what is going on in a particular country. Most information is gathered from newspapers and government reports. CIA officers are not like the spies seen on television and movies—and they are especially not like 007 James Bond.

To get secret information, officers recruit foreigners who are known as agents. CIA officers look for potential agents at restaurants, bars, evening social gatherings, and parties. They offer money or favors in exchange for information. For example, a CIA officer once offered heart medicine to an ailing Soviet ambassador, but the Soviet turned down the deal.

CIA officers use a **cover** that disguises the fact that they work for the CIA. Usually, they pose as U.S. government workers or as members of the U.S. military stationed abroad. CIA officers posing as government workers have diplomatic protection if they are caught spying or recruiting agents. When caught, they are generally ordered to go back to the United States and never to return. Other CIA officers pose as businessmen or as tourists. If they are caught spying, they can face serious penalties.

Each CIA station gathers information, writes it into reports, and sends it to the Directorate of Intelligence in Washington, D.C. If a report is urgent, it is coded *critic* or *flash*. Less important codes are *immediate*, *priority*, and *routine*. At the Directorate of Intelligence, experts pore over the reports and then write recommendations and make predictions. These recommendations are summarized in the President's Daily Brief, which is delivered every morning to the president of the United States. Using this information, the president and his advisors make decisions that affect millions of people around the world.

Spies All Around

The CIA claims that it spies on every nation in the world except for Canada, Great Britain, and Australia. Why? Sometimes it is important to know what your friends are doing as well as your enemies.

For example, the United States has pledged to protect Taiwan from a Chinese attack but has no desire to provoke a war with China. In 1988, the CIA learned that Taiwan was trying to build an atomic bomb. Knowing that China would attack if Taiwan had the bomb, U.S. officials told Taiwan to stop their work, and they did.

During the Cold War, the CIA worked with the FBI to recruit Soviet agents. They looked for signs that a KGB officer might be willing to work for U.S. intelligence. Once, the CIA found a KGB officer who seemed very interested in American culture, and he was later recruited.

One of the best ways to get information is to eavesdrop on a conversation. To do so, the CIA installs bugs—tiny microphones that broadcast sounds to a listening post—in many foreign government buildings. Often, officers must install the bugs by breaking into buildings, sometimes at night or after hours. Bugs can be a great source of information, but they can also be a waste of time. In one operation, officers bugged an

embassy in a Southeast Asian country. When they tried to listen, all they could hear were birds chirping!

Three Men in China

Some CIA officers spend years in jail or lose their lives in the line of duty. In the 1950s, Hugh Redmond, a veteran of World War II and a CIA officer in China, posed as a businessman and recruited agents in Shanghai. After China became a communist country, Redmond was arrested in 1951. Because he had no diplomatic cover, he was not released.

More CIA officers were captured. In November 1952, a U.S. airplane tried to drop paratroopers into China to aid rebels fighting the communist government. The plane was shot down, and two CIA officers on board, John T. Downey and Richard G. Fecteau, were taken prisoner. They joined Redmond in jail.

In 1958, the mothers of the three men finally were permitted to see them. After seven years in prison, Redmond still refused to confess that he was a CIA officer. Prison life was harsh. He had lost weight, his hair, and his teeth.

Redmond stayed in prison until 1970, when Chinese officials reported that he had slashed himself with a razor and had bled to death. His ashes were sent to his home in Yonkers,

CIA agent John T. Downey crosses over to freedom in Hong Kong after spending twenty years as a prisoner in China.

CIA director George J. Tenet and President George W. Bush stand in front of a memorial to CIA officials who lost their lives in service to their country. Each black star represents a deceased officer. This photograph was taken in March 2001.

New York. Fecteau was released in 1971 after eighteen years in prison. Downey came home two years later.

There is a memorial to CIA officers who have died during operations at the CIA headquarters in Langley, Virginia. Seventy-eight black stars, each representing a deceased officer, are chiseled into a slab of white marble. Below the wall

HOSE MEMBERS
TELLIGENCE AGENCY
SERVICE OF THEIR COUNTRY

of stars rests a book in a locked, bulletproof glass case. Forty-three names are written in the book. The remaining stars have no names. The CIA has not revealed the names of these individuals because their missions are still classified. Journalist Ted Gup, while researching his book *The Book of Honor*, discovered that one of the stars is for Hugh Redmond.

While it fought against communism abroad, the CIA defended charges that it had communists in its own ranks. In this cartoon, the bull—Senator Joseph McCarthy—is charging into the CIA "China Shop" while CIA director Allen Dulles cowers with President Eisenhower. In the early 1950s, McCarthy led an unsuccessful campaign to weed out communism in the U.S. government. Today this campaign is called McCarthyism.

A Visit to the China Shop

Chapter Four

Covert Action

Throughout the Cold War, the CIA was able to influence the economies and politics of other countries through covert action. To protect U.S. interests, CIA officers sent weapons, supplies, and money to groups that rebelled against communist regimes. In some cases, the officers trained these groups in warfare. Meanwhile, the Soviet Union ran its own secret operations.

Fighting for Europe

Both the Soviet Union and the United States spent billions of dollars to influence elections in Western Europe. After

World War II, the CIA was especially worried about Italy, whose communist party was the largest outside of the Soviet Union. Italy's 1948 election became a Cold War battleground.

The CIA threw its support behind the Christian Democrats, a moderate political group. During the elections, the CIA paid for posters and radio broadcasts that portrayed the Christian Democrats favorably. The agency also bribed newspaper editors to print good news about the Christian Democrats and bad news about the communists. The Christian Democrats—and the United States—won a crushing victory.

Members of the CIA-backed Christian Democrat Party distribute leaflets in Bologna, Italy, in April 1948.

Rebellion in Iran

In 1951, an Iranian man named Mohammed Mossadegh led a rebellion against the Iranian leader, Shah Reza Pahlevi. More alarming, Mossadegh permitted the existence of an Iranian communist party. To support the shah, the CIA sent agent Kermit "Kim" Roosevelt to Iran in June 1953. He traveled secretly into the capital city, Tehran, by hiding beneath a blanket on the floor of a car. Roosevelt urged the shah to call for Mossadegh's resignation. When the shah did so, however, riots exploded in the city streets. Panicked, the shah fled to Italy, and Mossadegh took power in Iran.

"The shah," said Roosevelt, "was a wimp."

Roosevelt now began an operation to support a rebellion against Mossadegh. With $10,000, he paid hundreds of people to stage a riot in support of the shah. As the group walked noisily through the streets, more and more Iranians joined them. Mossadegh was forced to flee. In Rome, the shah was delighted to learn that he ruled Iran once again.

President Eisenhower was also pleased. As a general in World War II, Eisenhower had seen firsthand the horrors of war. Iran was a virtually bloodless victory that had only cost money and very few lives.

Followers of the shah of Iran carry his portrait through the streets after the shah is restored to power in August 1953.

37

The "Perfect Failure"

In 1958, Fidel Castro seized power in Cuba, an island nation just 90 miles (145 km) away from Florida. When Castro became a communist and embraced the Soviet Union, the United States began to see Cuba as a major threat. Thus began the CIA's long involvement with Castro and Cuba, a source of some of the agency's worst embarrassments.

In the late 1950s, the CIA provided weapons and military training to Cuban exiles who had fled Castro. The agency planned an air attack that would destroy Castro's air force while the newly trained exile force swarmed ashore. The remaining Cuban people, it was planned, would then revolt against Castro. In 1961, CIA and U.S. military leaders urged the new president, John F. Kennedy, to order the attack. The inexperienced Kennedy agreed.

On April 15, 1961, planes flown by the exiles began bombing Cuba. The next night, the 1,500-man force left Nicaragua for the Bay of Pigs, a landing site on Cuba's southern coast. One day later, the ships arrived and the troops swam ashore. Castro was informed of the situation almost immediately. He ordered his air force to strike the ships while Cuban militia units surrounded the beach. Without supplies or air cover, the invaders were soon trapped. No uprising exploded from the Cuban people, and within one day, the invasion began to collapse.

In Washington, D.C., Kennedy watched the disaster unfold with horror. On April 18, Castro's troops wiped out the

Air America

To supply its operations all over the world, the CIA bought and operated airlines. The CIA used cover names to disguise the fact that the airlines worked for them. Companies with cover names such as Air America, Intermountain, and Civil Air Transport flew hundreds of missions. The planes carried men, equipment, and supplies to secret CIA operations around the world. The pilots were trained to fly low, just above jungles and mountain slopes. They learned to fly at night and in all kinds of weather.

Cuban rebel forces are captured by Castro's troops after the CIA-backed Bay of Pigs invasion in April 1961. This failed invasion was an enormous embarrassment to the United States.

invasion force, capturing 1,189 rebels and killing more than 100. Among the dead were four American pilots who had flown bombers during the attack.

For the United States, the disaster was total. One historian called it "a perfect failure." The United States was forced to pay $53 million worth of supplies and food for the return of the rebels. A humiliated Kennedy raged at the CIA, and several CIA leaders resigned. Until then, most Americans had

Trimming the Beard

After the failed Bay of Pigs invasion, the CIA concocted absurd schemes to get rid of Cuban leader Fidel Castro, whom they nicknamed "The Beard." One plan was to poison Castro's cigars. Another plan called for putting special chemicals in his shoes to make his hair fall out. Without his beard, thought some CIA leaders, Castro would lose his power. The agency even tried to hire criminals to kill Castro, but the plot failed. The Beard lives on today.

respected the agency. The Bay of Pigs became a symbol of CIA blundering.

Chile

In 1970, Salvador Allende won the presidential election in Chile. Because Allende once supported communism, the CIA

The CIA spent almost $8 million to help unseat Chilean president Salvador Allende, pictured here in Santiago just before he lost his position in 1973.

immediately took notice. During the next three years, the CIA spent nearly $8 million to unseat Allende. Some CIA officers were upset by this action because Chile had a tradition of democracy. Their concerns went unheeded.

Then, in 1973, a general named Augusto Pinochet took over the country in a move supported by the United States. Pinochet became one of the harshest and bloodiest leaders in Chilean history. When a U.S. Senate committee asked former CIA director Richard Helms if the agency had helped to destabilize Chile, Helms said no. In 1976, the public learned

The *Glomar Explorer*

On April 11, 1968, a Soviet submarine, *K-129,* was submerged in the Pacific Ocean. Then something went terribly wrong: the sub sank, plunging 16,500 feet (5,000 m) to the bottom of the ocean. The Soviets could not locate the sunken vessel, but the U.S. Navy heard an explosion on underwater microphones and knew the sub's location.

Four years later, the CIA began an incredible project. At a cost of at least $200 million, the CIA teamed up with a company headed by wealthy Hollywood filmmaker Howard Hughes to build *Glomar Explorer.* Hughes told reporters that the ship was designed to search the ocean depths for precious metals—but that was just the cover. Inside the 619-foot (189-m) ship was a special storage pool. The CIA planned to use *Glomar Explorer* to lift *K-129* off the ocean floor and to retrieve all of its codes, weapons, and technology.

On July 4, 1974, *Glomar Explorer* reached the spot above the sunken submarine. Slowly, a giant claw was lowered into the black depths. The claw closed around *K-129*'s hull and inched back to the surface. In a heart-stopping moment, one of the claws snapped, and a portion of the submarine sank back to the bottom. The rest was pulled into *Glomar Explorer.* The CIA recovered the forward piece of the submarine, which included encoding machines, two nuclear-tipped torpedoes, and the bodies of eight Soviet sailors. The sailors were buried with full honors at sea.

of the CIA's covert action to unseat Allende. A federal judge fined Helms $2,000 for lying to Congress.

The Church Hearings

By the middle of the 1970s, the CIA faced severe criticism. In a series of congressional hearings held in 1975, lawmakers stripped away the blanket of secrecy that had protected the CIA for so long, and they did not like what they found. Congress learned that the CIA had conducted drug experiments on people without their knowledge. The agency had opened mail sent to the Soviet Union and had spied on American

In the mid-1970s, Senator Frank Church led a congressional effort to investigate the CIA's illegal activities.

protest groups in the 1960s. Worst of all, it had authorized assassinations of leaders.

Senator Frank Church, the congressman in charge of the CIA Senate hearings, compared the CIA to a "rogue elephant rampaging out of control." The CIA was criticized for being too secretive and holding too much power. Many Americans believed that the agency's operations routinely broke the law.

The Church hearings caused great change within the agency. The CIA could no longer ignore Congress and run risky, illegal operations just because the president ordered them. Assassination was forbidden, and the CIA's budget and staff were cut.

President Ronald Reagan walks with CIA director William Casey in May 1984. The two men launched an international battle against communism.

Chapter Five

Into the Twenty-first Century

In 1980, the United States elected a new president, Ronald Reagan, who promised to get tough with the Soviets. Calling the Soviet Union an "evil empire," Reagan increased military spending. The CIA's budget and staff grew, and William Casey took over as director. Under Casey's direction, the CIA fought communists in Africa and Central America. For example,

after the Soviets invaded neighboring Afghanistan in 1979 just prior to Reagan's election, the CIA increased weapon shipments to the rebels resisting the invasion.

In the 1980s, the United States grappled with increased international terrorism. On April 18, 1983, a truck drove into the American embassy in Beirut, Lebanon, a city in the war-torn **Middle East**. The truck, packed with explosives, detonated. The blast ripped through the building. Among the seventeen Americans killed were seven CIA officers. In 1984, the head CIA officer in Beirut was kidnapped and murdered. Intelligence work abroad was becoming more dangerous.

Victory in the Persian Gulf

In July 1990, American satellites orbited hundreds of miles above the country of Iraq in the Middle East. The satellites took thousands of photographs that showed Iraqi tanks, supplies, and soldiers gathering along the border of a

Opposite: *The American Embassy in Beirut, Lebanon, is destroyed after a car bomb explodes on April 19, 1983.*

Still Watching

The CIA never stops watching for important intelligence. In 2001, the *New York Times* reported that CIA officers had been studying a novel supposedly written by Saddam Hussein. The officers hoped to find insights into Saddam's character.

smaller country called Kuwait. Iraqi leader Saddam Hussein assured President George Bush that he would pull his troops back, but Bush knew better because the CIA had warned him. As the CIA had predicted, the Iraqi armies stormed across Kuwait's border on August 1.

Bush moved quickly. He publicly condemned the attack and began assembling an army to drive Saddam out of Kuwait. The CIA played a critical role in the coming battles, known as the Persian Gulf War. CIA officers contacted businessmen who had worked in Iraq, found floor plans of Iraqi factories, recommended targets, and counted Iraqi tanks and battle units. They also created a radio station that urged Iraqi soldiers to surrender. When American pilots were shot down, the CIA worked to rescue them. In February 1991, the Persian Gulf War ended in victory for the United States and its allies.

Mole

The 1990s were also painful years for the CIA. In 1994, a CIA employee, Aldrich Ames, was arrested for passing secrets to the Russians. Ames, who had worked for the CIA for thirty-one years, had sold the agency's deepest secrets for $2.5 million. He had caused the deaths of at least ten Soviet and Russian agents and had revealed every CIA operation planned against the Soviets.

The Ames case showed the CIA as arrogant and flawed. Despite earning a modest salary, Ames owned a $540,000 house and drove a luxury car to work.

Former CIA officer Aldrich Ames leaves the U.S. District Court after being sentenced to life in prison. Ames took more than $2 million from the Russians in exchange for CIA secrets.

When the Federal Bureau of Investigation (FBI) became suspicious of Ames, the CIA refused to cooperate. Ames had failed five lie-detecting tests, but still the agency did nothing. When the Ames story was reported in the newspapers, no CIA officers were fired. Ames literally had sold the CIA—and the nation's security—to the Russians.

A Second Pearl Harbor

On the clear, sunny morning of September 11, 2001, terrorists hijacked four airliners in the skies above the United States. At about 8:45 A.M., one jet flew in low over New York City and slammed into the north tower of the World Trade Center. Another jet, approaching from the southwest, dove into the south tower. Within 2 hours, both towers had crumbled to the ground in an explosion of glass, smoke, dust, and pulverized concrete.

At almost exactly the same time, in Washington, D.C., another plane swooped over the city and crashed into the Pentagon, the headquarters of the nation's military. Over western Pennsylvania, passengers made frantic cell-phone calls to report that their plane had been hijacked. Minutes later, the airliner suddenly streaked downward and exploded in an empty field.

September 11, 2001, was a bloody day in American history. Almost three thousand people had been killed. Shocked and

President George W. Bush meets with his cabinet and advisors four days after the September 11, 2001, terrorist attacks. Clockwise from left: Attorney General John Ashcroft, Vice President Dick Cheney, President Bush, Secretary of State Colin Powell, Secretary of Defense Donald Rumsfeld, Deputy Secretary of Defense Paul Wolfowitz, FBI director Robert Mueller, Secretary of the Treasury Paul O'Neill, CIA director George J. Tenet, White House Chief of Staff Andy Card, National Security Advisor Condoleeza Rice, and General Henry H. Shelton, Chairman of the Joint Chiefs of Staff.

enraged, the nation's leaders wondered how they had been so surprised. One lawmaker and several journalists compared the disaster to Pearl Harbor. Once again, the CIA found itself under severe criticism for not providing any warning. It was also revealed that the CIA had been trying unsuccessfully to capture or kill Osama bin Laden, the suspected terrorist and mastermind of the September 11 tragedy, for years.

The CIA has played a critical role in the war against terrorism. The terrorist attacks brought home to Americans how important intelligence was. The agency deployed officers to Afghanistan to rally forces against the ruling Taliban regime, which was hiding and harboring bin Laden. Congress pledged more money to the intelligence community. A White House panel recommended that three Pentagon intelligence agencies be transferred to the CIA.

The disastrous attacks of September 11 once again reminded the United States of the need for a strong, well-funded intelligence agency. More than ever, it is the CIA's job to detect terrorist plots before they happen. This will ensure that a day like Pearl Harbor and September 11 never happens again.

Timeline

1941	Japan bombs Pearl Harbor; the United States enters World War II.
1942	General William "Wild Bill" Donovan forms the Office of Strategic Services.
1947	Congress passes the National Security Act, which creates the Central Intelligence Agency (CIA).
1950	The Korean War begins.
1953	The CIA helps restore the shah to power in Iran.
1956	The U-2 spy plane makes its first flight over the Soviet Union.
1959	The first Corona satellite is launched.
1960	The U-2 spy plane is shot down over the Soviet Union.
1961	The CIA suffers a major defeat at the Bay of Pigs, Cuba.
1960–1975	The CIA fights a covert war in Southeast Asia.
1974	*Glomar Explorer* raises the Soviet submarine *K-129*.
1975	Senator Frank Church establishes a committee to examine the CIA.
1980	President Ronald Reagan promises to get tough with the Soviets. The CIA begins supplying Afghanistanian rebels with weapons and fights communist groups in Central America.
1983	The American embassy is bombed in Beirut. Seven CIA officers die.
1990	Iraq invades Kuwait; after a U.S.-led buildup in the Persian Gulf, Iraqi armies are defeated.
1994	Aldrich Ames, a CIA employee who sold information to the Soviets and Russians, is uncovered.

Glossary

agent—a person who engages in secret activities to get information

bug—a device that broadcasts sound to a listening post; used to overhear conversations

classified—withheld from the public for reasons of national security; confidential

Cold War—a period of hostility between the United States and the Soviet Union that lasted from about 1945 to 1990. The war was "cold" because the two countries never fought directly with each other.

communist—following a political system or theory in which all property is owned and controlled by a central government

cover—a false name or disguise

covert action—operations done in secret to gather information about a foreign government or to overthrow a country's leaders

embassy—a building housing the ambassador of a government in a foreign country

espionage—the use of spies or covert action to get secret information

intelligence—information about another country, including its military, economy, and leaders

Middle East—the area of the world centered around Israel, Saudi Arabia, and Iraq

To Find Out More

Books

Binns, Tristan Boyer. *CIA: Central Intelligence Agency.* Chicago: Heinemann Libraries, 2002.

Gup, Ted. *The Book of Honor: The Secret Lives and Deaths of CIA Operatives.* New York: Random House, 2000.

Kessler, Ronald. *Inside the CIA.* New York: Simon & Schuster, 1992.

Thomas, Evan. *The Very Best Men: Four Who Dared: The Early Years of the CIA.* New York: Simon & Schuster, 1996.

Organizations and Online Sites

The CIA's Homepage for Kids
http://www.odci.gov/cia/ciakids/index.html
This page is part of the official CIA Web site. It gives young readers information about the CIA.

Spy-Fi Archives
http://www.cia.gov/spy_fi/
This Web page gives a tour of a collection of spy equipment and posters depicting how the CIA has been portrayed in movies.

www.cia.gov
The official homepage of the Central Intelligence Agency.

Videos

CIA Secret Files. A & E, 1993.

Secrets of the CIA. Turner Original Productions, 1998.

The CIA: 50 Years of Spying. The History Channel, 1999.

A Note on Sources

To research this book, I read several books and articles, both in magazines and online. I found several to be particularly helpful. Ted Gup has written an excellent book on the CIA, *The Book of Honor*. In telling the tragic stories of CIA officers who were killed on missions, Gup gives an intimate view of how the CIA actually operated. Ronald Kessler's *Inside the CIA* is packed with information and stories. *The Ultimate Spy Book*, by H. Keith Melton, is an extensive review of the tools of espionage. *A Century of Spies* is a survey of notorious spies during the last century. *The Very Best Men* is a very readable account of the CIA's early years and the men who ran it.

—*Brendan January*

Index

Numbers in *italics* indicate illustrations.

About the Author

Brendan January is an award-winning author of more than twenty nonfiction books for young readers. He is a graduate of Haverford College, Pennsylvania, and Columbia Graduate School of Journalism. January is currently a journalist at *The Record* in Bergen County, New Jersey. He lives with his wife in Jersey City.